Explore San
Ang

A Travel Guide Top Attractions, Hidden Gems, and Local Tips for an Unforgettable Adventure.

George B. Lawson

All rights reserved. No part of this publication may be reproduced, distributed, or transmitted in any form or by any means, including photocopying, recording, or other electronic or mechanical methods, without the prior written permission of the publisher, except in the case of brief quotations embodied in critical reviews and certain other noncommercial uses permitted by copyright law.

Copyright ©George B. Lawson, 2025.

Table of Contents

Introduction 6
  Overview of San Francisco and Los Angeles 6
    Why San Francisco and LA Are Must-Visit Destinations 8
  Best Time to Visit: Weather, Events, and Crowd Considerations 10
    San Francisco: Seasonal Weather Patterns 10
    Spring (March to May) 10
    Summer (June to August): 11
    Fall (September to November): 12
    Los Angeles: Seasonal Weather Patterns 14
Part I: San Francisco - The City by the Bay 19
  Top Landmarks & Attractions 20
  Cultural and Artistic Gems 27
    SFMOMA (San Francisco Museum of Modern Art) 27
    Must-See Exhibits & Programs: 28
  California Academy of Sciences: 29
  Exploratorium: 31
  Neighborhoods to Explore 33
  Mission District: 33
  Haight-Ashbury: 35

- North Beach: 38
- Nature and Day Trips 39
- Muir Woods 40
- Point Reyes: 41
- Land End and Golden Gate Park: 43
- Hidden Gems and Local Favorites 45
- Dolores Park: 46
- Twin Peaks 48
- Ferry Building Marketplace: 50

Cultural and Artistic Hotspots 53
- The Getty Center. 53
- LACMA (Los Angeles County Museum of Art). 56
- Top Neighborhoods to Visit 59
  - Venice Beach. 59
  - Beverly Hills. 61
  - Downtown LA 63
- Nature and Day Trips 66
  - Malibu 66
  - Santa Barbara 68
  - San Diego 70
- Local Tips and Hidden Spots 72
  - El Matador Beach 72
  - The Last Bookstore 73

- LACMA's Urban Light 74
- Getting There 77
  - The best flight options to both cities 77
    - Top airlines and tips for finding deals 77
    - Transportation Within the Cities 79
  - Accommodations 82
    - San Francisco: Recommended Neighborhoods to Stay In 82
  - Packing Essentials 89
- Part IV: Food & Dining 96
  - Food & Dining 97
    - Must-Try Foods in San Francisco 97
    - Must-Try Foods in Los Angeles 99
    - Dining Tips 101
- Part V: Itineraries 104
  - Itineraries 105
  - 3-Day Itinerary for San Francisco 105
    - 3-Day Itinerary for Los Angeles 107
    - 1-Week Itinerary for Both Cities 109
- Travel Planners & Maps. 111

Introduction

Overview of San Francisco and Los Angeles

San Francisco and Los Angeles, two of California's most iconic cities, each hold their own special allure. Whether you're captivated by San Francisco's steep hills, historic cable cars, and scenic waterfront or enchanted by the Hollywood glamour and sun-soaked beaches of Los Angeles, these cities offer something for everyone.

San Francisco is a city of breathtaking contrasts—where Victorian houses stand in the shadow of ultra-modern skyscrapers, and fog often rolls in to soften the golden light. Known for its compact size and stunning landscapes, San Francisco boasts a unique blend of natural beauty, cultural diversity, and a progressive spirit. The city is defined by its iconic landmarks like the Golden Gate Bridge and Alcatraz Island, but it also thrives in the energy of its eclectic neighborhoods, such as the hip Mission District or the historic Chinatown. With its hilly streets, frequent fog, and proximity to both the Pacific Ocean and redwood forests, the geography here is nothing short of stunning.

Los Angeles, on the other hand, is an expansive metropolis defined by its sprawling urban landscape, palm-lined streets, and a year-round sunny climate. LA, often referred to as the entertainment capital of the world, draws visitors from every corner of the globe with its connection to Hollywood, iconic beaches, and vibrant cultural scenes. It's a city that pulses with creativity—where movie stars, musicians, and artists have made their mark, and where the pace of life is as fast as the traffic. From the beaches of Venice and Santa Monica to the nightlife of Downtown LA, the city offers a world of opportunity for those seeking a mix of laid-back vibes and high-energy exploration.

The geography of both cities couldn't be more different. San Francisco sits on a series of steep hills along the bay, its terrain characterized by narrow streets and stunning waterfront views. Los Angeles is built in a valley, with mountain ranges to the north and endless stretches of coastline to the south. LA is a sprawling city, where attractions like Universal Studios, Griffith Park, and Malibu's beaches are spread out across the urban sprawl.

The history of both cities is rich and varied. San Francisco's story is inextricably tied to the California Gold Rush of the mid-1800s, which helped transform it into a major port city. Over the years, the city has grown into a cultural hub known for its tolerance, acceptance, and progressive values. Los Angeles, though settled earlier in 1781 by Spanish colonists, rose to prominence in the late 19th century with the discovery of oil and later became a booming center for the film industry in the early 20th century. While San Francisco's charm is tied to its vintage, old-world feel, Los Angeles pulses with modernity, creativity, and a never-ending sense of reinvention.

Why San Francisco and LA Are Must-Visit Destinations

San Francisco and Los Angeles are among the most sought-after destinations in the United States, and for good reason. Each city has its own story to tell, with a mix of cultural experiences, iconic landmarks, and unique vibes that make them stand out.

San Francisco is a city that captures the heart with its stunning views, iconic landmarks, and rich history. From walking across the Golden Gate Bridge to exploring the depths of Alcatraz, every corner of San Francisco feels like a discovery. The city's neighborhoods each have their own charm, from the vibrant and artsy Mission District to the historic and bustling Fisherman's Wharf. It's a place where you can ride a cable car up steep hills and walk through historic streets, while enjoying the beauty of the Pacific Ocean and the nearby Bay Area.

Los Angeles, with its sunny weather and star-studded reputation, is another must-see destination. It's the city where dreams are made—whether it's the dream of becoming a Hollywood star or the dream of lounging on a palm-fringed beach. LA is all about living big, and that energy extends from its gorgeous beaches like Venice and Malibu to its dazzling landmarks like the Hollywood Walk of Fame and the famous Griffith Observatory. The cultural scene is unmatched, from the Getty Center's incredible art collection to the glitz and glamour of the Oscars. LA is also known for its diverse food scene, featuring flavors from every part of the world.

What really sets both cities apart is their vibrant neighborhoods. San Francisco's diversity is evident in its neighborhoods—each with a distinct personality. From the counterculture of Haight-Ashbury to the old-world charm of Chinatown, San Francisco is a city that feels like it has many different personalities, all coexisting within a few miles of each other. In contrast, LA's neighborhoods stretch far and wide, each offering a different taste of the city. Venice Beach offers a quirky, artistic vibe, while Beverly Hills showcases luxury and glamour. LA's many identities—from beach town to urban metropolis—make it a truly unique place.

One of the best parts of visiting these cities is the opportunity to mix sightseeing with personal stories. For instance, you may find yourself enjoying a peaceful moment on the Golden Gate Bridge, like one traveler I met who told me how the bridge reminded him of the freedom he felt when traveling solo across the U.S. Or, you might experience the excitement of standing at the top of Runyon Canyon in LA, as I did during my first trip, when the city stretched out before me in all its sprawling glory.

Best Time to Visit: Weather, Events, and Crowd Considerations.

When planning a trip to San Francisco and Los Angeles, understanding the seasonal weather patterns, local events, and crowd considerations is essential to maximizing your travel experience. The timing of your visit will impact everything from what to pack to the types of activities you can enjoy and the crowds you may encounter. Here's an in-depth look at what to expect during different seasons in both cities:

San Francisco: Seasonal Weather Patterns

San Francisco's weather is famously unpredictable, with fog often rolling in from the Pacific Ocean. The city's microclimates can mean that different parts of the city experience vastly different weather on the same day. Here's what you can expect during each season:

Spring (March to May)

Weather: Spring in San Francisco is often mild, but it can still be chilly, especially in the mornings and evenings. Daytime temperatures range from 55°F to 70°F (13°C to 21°C), and while there is less fog than in the summer, it's still common, particularly near the Golden Gate Bridge.

What to Pack: Layering is key during spring. Bring a light jacket, sweaters, and comfortable shoes for walking, as you may encounter some cool, windy days.

Things to Do: Spring is one of the best times to visit for outdoor activities. The weather is generally pleasant for sightseeing, with fewer tourists compared to summer. You can explore Golden Gate Park, take a ferry to Alcatraz Island, or visit Muir Woods National Monument to see the redwoods.

Events: Key events during this time include the San Francisco International Film Festival (April-May) and the Cherry Blossom Festival (April), which showcases the city's Japanese culture and traditions.

Summer (June to August):

Weather: Summer in San Francisco is known for its cooler-than-expected temperatures. Daytime highs typically range between 60°F and 70°F (16°C to 21°C), but it can feel much colder in coastal areas due to the fog. Expect cooler evenings and mornings, with temperatures dipping into the 50s (10°C).

What to Pack: Summer requires layers—bring a light jacket, scarves, and sturdy shoes for walking. A sweater or hoodie is a must for early mornings and evenings.

Things to Do: Despite the fog, summer offers the best weather for outdoor adventures in San Francisco.

You can enjoy walks along the Embarcadero, ride a bike across the Golden Gate Bridge, or take a boat cruise around the bay. Visiting the Fisherman's Wharf area is also a great option as you'll find lively shops and delicious seafood restaurants.

Events: Bay to Breakers (May) is one of the city's quirkiest events, a fun run filled with participants dressed in outrageous costumes. The San Francisco Pride Parade (June) is another colorful event that fills the streets with celebrations of diversity and inclusivity. If you're interested in music, check out the Outside Lands Music and Arts Festival (August), held in Golden Gate Park.

Fall (September to November):

Weather: Fall is often the best time to visit San Francisco because it offers the city's warmest weather. Temperatures can range from 60°F to 75°F (16°C to 24°C), and the fog begins to dissipate, giving way to clearer skies. It's a fantastic time to explore the city's outdoor spaces.

What to Pack: Fall's mild temperatures make it perfect for casual attire, such as light jackets or sweaters, jeans, and comfortable shoes.

Things to Do: Fall is ideal for sightseeing without the summer crowds. Visit the Golden Gate Bridge, go hiking at Land End, or spend time enjoying the waterfront at Crissy Field. Biking is another great way to see the city in fall, as temperatures are comfortable and the streets are less crowded.

- Events: Fall hosts many great cultural festivals and events, such as Fleet Week (October), featuring a spectacular air show and military exhibits, and the Hardly Strictly Bluegrass Festival (October), a free music festival held in Golden Gate Park. Halloween also brings various fun events, including Ghost Walks around the city.

4. Winter (December to February):

- Weather: Winters in San Francisco are mild, with average highs between 50°F and 60°F (10°C to 15°C). The fog is often more prevalent in the winter months, particularly in the mornings. Rain is occasional, but not a daily occurrence.

- What to Pack: Pack for cooler temperatures, with jackets and layers. Be prepared for rain with a waterproof jacket or umbrella.

- Things to Do: Winter is a quieter time for tourists, so it's an excellent opportunity to enjoy the city at a slower pace. Explore the Musee Mecanique at Fisherman's Wharf, spend a day at the California Academy of Sciences, or check out the Palace of Fine Arts for a more peaceful experience.

- Events: Winter brings the San Francisco Ballet's Nutcracker (December), a holiday classic, and New Year's Eve Fireworks over the bay, offering spectacular views of the city skyline.

Los Angeles: Seasonal Weather Patterns

Los Angeles enjoys a much warmer and sunnier climate, with its consistent, year-round sunshine making it a popular destination throughout the year. Here's what to expect during each season:

1. Spring (March to May):

- Weather: Spring in Los Angeles is mild and pleasant, with temperatures ranging from 60°F to 75°F (16°C to 24°C). It's one of the best times to visit as the weather is neither too hot nor too cold, making it perfect for outdoor exploration.
- What to Pack: Spring in LA calls for light layers, such as t-shirts, light jackets, and comfortable walking shoes. Don't forget sunscreen, as the sun is often out.
- Things to Do: Spring is the perfect time for outdoor activities. Visit the Griffith Observatory, hike to the Hollywood Sign, or take a stroll along the Santa Monica Pier. You can also enjoy the Los Angeles County

Museum of Art (LACMA) or catch a live performance in the city.
- Events: LA hosts the LA Film Festival (April), the CicLAvia (April and May), where parts of the city are closed to cars for a day of biking, walking, and activities, and Coachella (April), an iconic music festival located just outside the city.

2. Summer (June to August):
   - Weather: LA's summer weather can be hot, especially in the inland areas, with temperatures frequently climbing above 85°F (29°C), though coastal areas like Santa Monica stay cooler. Expect long, sunny days and a lively atmosphere.
   - What to Pack: For hot weather, pack lightweight clothing like shorts, t-shirts, sun hats, and sunglasses. A light jacket for cooler evenings along the coast might also be necessary.
   - Things to Do: Summer is perfect for beach activities at Venice Beach and Santa Monica, visiting iconic locations like Hollywood Boulevard, or attending a Dodgers game at Dodger Stadium. It's also the season for exploring LA's vibrant neighborhoods, such as Downtown LA and Beverly Hills.

- Events: LA's Summer Music Concerts at places like the Hollywood Bowl, the LA County Fair (September), and the LA Pride Parade (June) offer unforgettable experiences. If you're a film lover, E3 Expo (June), the world's premier video game industry event, also happens during this time.

3. Fall (September to November):

    - Weather: Fall offers the most perfect weather in LA, with daytime temperatures ranging from 65°F to 80°F (18°C to 27°C). The summer heat starts to taper off, making it ideal for outdoor activities.

    - What to Pack: The mild temperatures allow you to pack light layers, with warm-weather clothing still appropriate for daytime, while a light jacket or sweater may be necessary for the cooler evenings.

    - Things to Do: Enjoy hikes in the Santa Monica Mountains, visit the Getty Center for world-class art, or take a tour of Universal Studios for an all-day adventure.

    - Events: Fall is packed with exciting events like Halloween Horror Nights at Universal Studios (September-October), the Los Angeles County Fair (September), and the Day of the Dead celebrations (October-November) in LA's cultural districts.

4. Winter (December to February):

- Weather: Mild is the best way to describe LA's winter weather. Average highs are between 60°F and 70°F (15°C to 21°C), and it rarely gets colder. Nights can be chilly, but snow is almost unheard of.

- What to Pack: Pack warm layers for the evenings, but light clothing is sufficient for daytime. Consider packing a rain jacket, as winter is the rainy season in LA.

- Things to Do: Winter is a quieter time to visit LA, so you can enjoy popular attractions like the Los Angeles County Museum of Art (LACMA) and Griffith Observatory without the summer crowds. You might also want to explore the Los Angeles Auto Show (December) or enjoy holiday festivities in Santa Monica and The Grove.

- Events: LA's New Year's Eve celebrations, Hollywood Christmas Parade (November-December), and LA's Ballet & Nutcracker performance (December) bring festive cheer to the city during winter months.

Which Time is Best for You?

- For the best weather: Fall in San Francisco and spring in Los Angeles are the top picks, with comfortable temperatures and fewer tourists.

- For the liveliest atmosphere: Summer brings the most energy to both cities, though be prepared for crowds.
- For budget-conscious travelers: Winter in both cities brings fewer tourists, meaning you'll likely get better hotel deals, but keep in mind some outdoor activities may be limited by rain or cooler temperatures.

By considering these seasonal variations, you can tailor your trip to enjoy the best weather, events, and experiences San Francisco and LA have to offer.

Part I: San Francisco - The City by the Bay

Top Landmarks & Attractions

Golden Gate Bridge: Why is it one of the most photographed structures in the world? What are the best vantage points for views and photos?

The Golden Gate Bridge is one of the most iconic landmarks not just in San Francisco, but in the world. It has become a symbol of the city, admired for both its engineering marvel and its breathtaking beauty. Spanning 1.7 miles, the bridge connects San Francisco to Marin County and is known for its distinct International Orange color, which contrasts dramatically with the often skies and deep blue waters below.

The Golden Gate Bridge is one of the most photographed structures in the world because of its dramatic setting: standing as an entrance to the San Francisco Bay. The combination of natural beauty with the modern elegance of the bridge creates a compelling visual, making it a favorite for photographers, artists, and travelers. Whether it's a sunlit morning, a foggy afternoon, or a sunset, the view changes with the weather, offering endless opportunities for striking photos.

Best Vantage Points for Views and Photos:

Battery Spencer: Located on the Marin side of the bridge, this viewpoint offers stunning views of the Golden Gate Bridge and San Francisco skyline, especially at sunrise or sunset. It's a short hike from the parking area, but well worth it for the perfect shot.

Crissy Field: This waterfront area in the Presidio is one of the best places for panoramic views of the bridge, especially if you want to capture the structure with the Bay and city skyline in the background. It's a great spot for a picnic and casual stroll along the beach.

Fort Point National Historic Site: Situated directly under the Golden Gate Bridge on the San Francisco side, this site provides a unique perspective, showcasing the bridge's architecture from below. It's a particularly great vantage point for capturing the bridge in all its grandeur.

Golden Gate Overlook: Located in the Presidio, this viewpoint offers one of the best views of the bridge and the bay, particularly during early morning hours when the fog is still rolling over the waters.

Alcatraz Island: What makes this former prison a popular tourist destination? What are the most compelling stories tied to it?

Alcatraz Island, located in the middle of the San Francisco Bay, is one of the most famous former prisons in the world. The island has a long history, from being a military fortification in the 1800s to becoming a high-security federal penitentiary in the

20th century. But what really makes Alcatraz stand out as a popular tourist destination are the gripping stories tied to its time as a prison.

Alcatraz was home to some of the most notorious criminals in American history, including Al Capone and Robert Stroud, known as the "Birdman of Alcatraz." The prison, which operated from 1934 to 1963, was known for its harsh conditions and isolation from the mainland. The infamous escape attempts have long captivated the public's imagination, with the most famous being the 1962 escape by three inmates—Frank Morris and the Anglin brothers—who were never found, sparking rumors that they may have made it to freedom. Their escape was immortalized in the Clint Eastwood film *Escape from Alcatraz*.

Visitors can take a self-guided audio tour of the prison to hear firsthand accounts from former guards and inmates about life inside. The cold, dark cells, solitary confinement, and the challenging weather conditions on the island give a stark reminder of the prison's grim reality. But it's also a site of fascinating history, having been the site of a Native American occupation in the late 1960s when activists sought to draw attention to issues affecting indigenous communities.

Compelling Stories:

The Escape of 1962: The escape attempt by Frank Morris and the Anglin brothers is perhaps one of the most intriguing mysteries of Alcatraz. They carved holes in their cells, created lifelike mannequins to fool guards, and escaped through the prison's sewer system and onto the water, never to be found again.

The Native American Occupation (1969-1971): After the prison closed, the island was taken over by Native American activists who wanted to raise awareness about their rights and living conditions. This peaceful occupation eventually led to the establishment of a Native American museum on the island today.

Fisherman's Wharf: What's the atmosphere here, and what can visitors expect? Which spots offer the best seafood and views of the bay?

Fisherman's Wharf is one of San Francisco's most popular tourist destinations, offering a lively, bustling atmosphere that captures the essence of the city's waterfront. Historically, it was the heart of San Francisco's fishing industry, but today, it's an area filled with shops, seafood restaurants, street performers, and scenic views of the San Francisco Bay.

Visitors can expect to see street vendors offering crab chowder, fresh fish, and other seafood delights, while watching boats come and go from the harbor. The area is home to some of the city's most iconic spots, including the famous Pier 39, a waterfront shopping center that offers unique boutiques, attractions, and views of the water. Pier 39 is also known for its sea lion colony, which has taken over the docks in recent years and is a fun attraction to watch.

Best Seafood Spots and Views:

- Boudin Bakery: Famous for its sourdough bread, this bakery also serves a hearty clam chowder in a sourdough bowl, a quintessential San Francisco meal that's beloved by locals and tourists alike.

- Alioto's: One of the oldest seafood restaurants at Fisherman's Wharf, Alioto's serves fresh crab, calamari, and other seafood dishes with beautiful views of the water and the Bay.

- Scoma's: Located on the water, Scoma's offers an exceptional dining experience with a menu of fresh, local seafood and stunning views of the bay, making it a favorite for a relaxed meal by the water.

Chinatown: What are the cultural highlights of San Francisco's Chinatown? Why is it a unique destination compared to others across the US?

San Francisco's Chinatown is not only the oldest in North America but also the largest outside of Asia. The neighborhood offers a fascinating blend of traditional Chinese culture mixed with San Francisco's unique urban energy. Stepping into Chinatown feels like entering another world, with narrow alleys, colorful markets, and the constant hum of activity. The area is famous for its bustling streets, herbal medicine shops, gold shops, and vibrant festivals.

What makes Chinatown truly unique is its rich history and cultural heritage. It's been home to generations of Chinese immigrants who've shaped the city's cultural fabric. From traditional Chinese New Year celebrations to ancient herbal remedies and the artistry of Chinese calligraphy, Chinatown offers a deep dive into the rich traditions of China, while blending seamlessly with the multicultural backdrop of San Francisco.

Cultural Highlights:

- The Dragon Gate: Located at the entrance to Chinatown on Grant Avenue, this iconic structure marks the entrance into the neighborhood and is a great place to begin your exploration.

- Golden Gate Fortune Cookie Factory: Step inside this tiny factory to see how traditional fortune cookies are made by hand. It's an interactive and fun stop, especially for those interested in the history of the beloved cookie.
- Chinese Temples and Shops: Explore traditional Buddhist temples and visit the herbal shops that line the streets. Chinatown is filled with places that have been passed down through generations, offering unique souvenirs and local goods.

Why It's Unique Compared to Other U.S. Chinatowns: San Francisco's Chinatown stands apart because of its historical significance, being the birthplace of many traditions that have spread across the country. The neighborhood's historic architecture, vibrant festivals like Chinese New Year, and the close-knit community make it a living testament to Chinese culture. Plus, it's located within walking distance of other iconic San Francisco neighborhoods, making it an accessible cultural gem.

Cultural and Artistic Gems

San Francisco is not only known for its stunning views and iconic landmarks, but it also boasts a thriving arts and culture scene. Whether you're an art enthusiast or simply curious about science and nature, the city offers a variety of world-class museums that are essential to understanding its creative and intellectual spirit. Here are some of the must-see cultural and artistic gems in the city:

SFMOMA (San Francisco Museum of Modern Art)

The San Francisco Museum of Modern Art (SFMOMA) is one of the largest and most innovative modern art museums in the country, making it a must-visit destination for any visitor with an interest in contemporary art. With over 33,000 pieces in its collection, SFMOMA houses works by iconic artists such as Andy Warhol, Frida Kahlo, Jackson Pollock, and Mark Rothko, as well as cutting-edge installations and exhibitions from both renowned and emerging artists.

Why SFMOMA is Essential:

World-Class Collection: With its vast collection of over 33,000 pieces, SFMOMA offers an unparalleled glimpse into the world of modern art. From paintings and sculptures to photographs, video art, and even immersive installations, it's a comprehensive look at the evolution of contemporary art.

Architectural Wonder: The museum itself is a work of art. The building, designed by Mario Botta and expanded by Snøhetta, is a masterpiece of modern architecture, combining sleek, open spaces with breathtaking views of the city and bay. The Patricia's Garden on the roof is a lovely spot to relax and take in the views of downtown San Francisco.

Inspiring Exhibitions and Events: The museum is constantly evolving, hosting groundbreaking exhibitions that explore a wide range of artistic practices. Visitors can enjoy immersive art experiences, like Ragnar Kjartansson's video installations or Barbara Kruger's thought-provoking visual statements. The rotating exhibitions ensure there's always something fresh and exciting to discover.

Must-See Exhibits & Programs:

"Seeing the Unseen" (Recent Exhibitions): This exhibit focuses on works that explore hidden, invisible, or abstract elements of life. It's a chance to reflect on how art can provoke thought and challenge perception.

- Warhol & Other Icons: The museum features a permanent collection of Andy Warhol's famous works, including his well-known Campbell's Soup Can and Marilyn Monroe series, along with collections by Roy

Lichtenstein, Jackson Pollock, and Jeff Koons. These exhibitions celebrate the pop art movement and its lasting impact.

- Interactive Programs: SFMOMA is also home to educational programs and workshops that allow visitors to interact with the art and even create their own. Check their calendar for hands-on activities like Family Days and Art Labs.

California Academy of Sciences:

What makes this museum essential for any visitor? What exhibits or programs are must-sees?

The California Academy of Sciences is one of the most spectacular natural history museums in the world and is a must-see for anyone visiting San Francisco. Located in Golden Gate Park, this museum is a haven for nature lovers, science enthusiasts, and families alike. It brings together diverse aspects of nature and science under one roof, with exhibits ranging from oceanography and paleontology to astronomy and environmental science.

Why California Academy of Sciences is Essential.

Unique and Interactive Exhibits: The museum offers an experience unlike any other. With a living roof, Amazon rainforest exhibit, and planetarium, it blends natural wonders and cutting-edge science. It's a place where you can explore everything from the depths of the oceans to the stars above.

Sustainable Design: One of the Academy's highlights is its green architecture, with the museum's roof covered in native plants, which not only helps the environment but also offers a unique design element that integrates with the surrounding park landscape.

Family-Friendly Learning: This museum is a dream for families, with engaging exhibits that make learning about the world around us both fun and educational. Whether you're walking through a recreated Amazon rainforest or looking at ancient fossils, there's something for everyone.

Must-See Exhibits & Programs:

The Living Roof: Take in panoramic views of Golden Gate Park while learning about the sustainable design of the building. This green roof is home to native plants and serves as an example of environmentally conscious architecture.

Rainforest and Aquarium: The Living Roof leads into the Rainforest Exhibit, a climate-controlled habitat that recreates a tropical rainforest. Visitors can walk through the different levels of the rainforest, surrounded by free-flying birds, butterflies, and lush greenery. The Steinhart Aquarium showcases aquatic life, including jellyfish, sea otters, and vibrant coral reefs.

Morrison Planetarium: This is one of the world's largest digital domes, offering immersive, interactive shows that bring the cosmos to life. You can take a journey to the edge of the universe, explore the night sky, or understand how we are connected to the stars in ways you never imagined.

Exploratorium:

How can this interactive science museum spark creativity and curiosity for travelers of all ages?

The Exploratorium is one of the most exciting and hands-on museums you can visit in San Francisco. Located on the Embarcadero, right on the waterfront, this interactive museum is a playground for curious minds, offering hundreds of exhibits that invite visitors to explore science, art, and human perception in an engaging and immersive way.

Why Exploratorium is Essential:

Hands-On Experience: Unlike most traditional museums where you simply look at exhibits, the Exploratorium allows you to touch, feel, and experiment with science. Every corner of the museum is designed to ignite curiosity and inspire discovery through play.

Innovative Exhibits: The Exploratorium is all about creativity and exploration, with exhibits that challenge visitors to think critically and interact with scientific principles. It's the perfect place for travelers of all ages, from young children to adults, to learn through engaging, hands-on experiences.

Situated by the Bay: The location of the Exploratorium, right along the water, gives it a picturesque backdrop with views of the San Francisco Bay and the Golden Gate Bridge.

How It Sparks Creativity and Curiosity:

Interactive Science: Exhibits like the Tactile Dome, where you must navigate an obstacle course in the dark, challenge your senses and encourage you to rethink your perception. It's a great way to engage your brain while having fun.

Living Systems and Art: The museum also blends art and science in unique ways, allowing visitors to create their own exhibits. One of the museum's signature features is its "Art and Perception" section, where you can experiment with how your mind interprets color, shape, and motion.

Outdoor Explorations: In addition to its indoor exhibits, the Exploratorium also has outdoor science exhibits that engage visitors with the environment.

Here, you can play with wind machines, kinetic sculptures, and interactive water displays.

Neighborhoods to Explore

San Francisco is a city of diverse neighborhoods, each with its own unique vibe and character. While many visitors flock to the well-known attractions, some of the most memorable experiences can be found by exploring these distinct, culturally rich areas. Whether you're interested in street art, history, or delicious food, here are three of the city's most fascinating neighborhoods: Mission District, Haight-Ashbury, and North Beach.

Mission District:

The Mission District is one of San Francisco's most dynamic neighborhoods, full of colorful murals, historic buildings, and a thriving food scene. It's a place where the old and the new coexist in a vibrant, ever-changing way. Known for its diverse culture, the Mission has been the heart of the city's Latino community for years, but its eclectic vibe now draws people from all walks of life.

Hidden Gems:

- Balmy Alley: This alley is a street art haven and one of the best places in the city to explore murals. Balmy Alley is a collection of vibrant murals that highlight social and political issues, often touching on themes of immigration, Chicano culture, and community activism. It's a must-visit for anyone wanting to experience the artistic soul of the Mission.

- The Secret Alley: This spot is tucked away in an industrial building off Mission Street and features a rotating collection of art installations, light sculptures, and creative exhibitions. It's an intimate, hidden treasure for art lovers.

- El Rio: A local institution, this unassuming bar has a fabulous outdoor patio where locals gather for live music, happy hours, and a laid-back atmosphere. It's one of those spots where you can truly soak in the neighborhood's energy.

Street Art:

- Clarion Alley: Another well-known spot for murals, Clarion Alley is covered in colorful, thought-provoking artwork, with new pieces constantly being added. The alley often hosts art shows and street performances, making it an ideal place for those interested in San Francisco's ever-evolving art scene.

Food Spots:

- La Taqueria: Known as the birthplace of San Francisco's famous mission-style burrito, La Taqueria serves up some of the city's best Mexican food. The carne asada burrito is a favorite among locals.

- Bi-Rite Creamery: A sweet spot in the Mission, Bi-Rite is famous for its artisan ice cream made from organic ingredients. Try the salted caramel flavor for a unique twist on a classic dessert.

- Taco Guerrero: This taco spot is a hidden gem, offering delicious, authentic street tacos at a reasonable price. It's perfect for grabbing a quick bite while wandering through the neighborhood.

Haight-Ashbury:

Haight-Ashbury is synonymous with the 1960s counterculture movement, making it one of the most historically significant neighborhoods in San Francisco. The area was the heart of the Summer of Love in 1967, when thousands of young people gathered here to protest the establishment, embrace new forms of art, and promote peace, love, and equality. Today, Haight-Ashbury still retains much of its bohemian charm, with vintage shops, eclectic cafes, and a laid-back atmosphere.

Counterculture History:

- The Summer of Love: Haight-Ashbury was the epicenter of the Summer of Love, a pivotal moment in history where thousands of young people from around the world came to San Francisco to engage in political activism, alternative lifestyles, and experimentation with art and music. Visitors can learn about this period by checking out the Haight-Ashbury neighborhood walking tour or visiting the Red Victorian Bed & Breakfast, which was once a gathering spot for writers and activists.

- The Diggers and Free Speech: The Digger movement and the call for free speech emerged in Haight-Ashbury during the 1960s. The Diggers, a collective of artists, ran free stores, organized events, and fought for the freedom of expression. The Haight-Ashbury History Center is a great place to explore more about this influential part of the neighborhood's history.

Notable Sites:

- The Red Victorian Bed & Breakfast: A historic building that served as a center for bohemian thinkers and artists in the 1960s. Today, it offers accommodations and a café, but its history as part of the counterculture movement is still evident.

- The Painted Ladies: Though not part of the counterculture movement directly, the Painted Ladies (the colorful Victorian houses across from Alamo Square Park) are a beautiful reminder of the city's rich architectural history and have been made famous in TV shows and movies, such as *Full House*.

Local Flavor:

- Amoeba Music: This legendary record store is one of the best places to explore Haight-Ashbury's musical history. You'll find an impressive selection of vinyl records, CDs, and music memorabilia from the 60s through to the present day.

- Haight Street Shops: Browse through the many vintage clothing stores, alternative bookshops, and quirky boutiques that line the street. You'll find everything from tie-dye shirts to rare books and local artisan goods.

- Psychedelic SF Tour: For those interested in learning more about the neighborhood's connection to the psychedelic movement, this guided tour explores the spiritual and artistic revolutions that unfolded here.

North Beach:

North Beach is San Francisco's Italian district, renowned for its cozy cafes, fine dining, and deep cultural roots. The neighborhood's proximity to the wharves and its vibrant nightlife make it one of the city's most popular areas to explore. Historically, it has been a hub for Italian immigrants, but over the years, it has also become the center of San Francisco's literary scene and a hotspot for Italian cuisine.

Exploring North Beach:

- Washington Square Park: The heart of North Beach, this green space is a great starting point for exploring the neighborhood. Surrounded by cafes and eateries, it's a place to relax and enjoy the local atmosphere. The Saints Peter and Paul Church, with its towering spires, is an iconic sight across from the park and a reminder of the neighborhood's Italian heritage.

- The Beat Generation Legacy: North Beach is also known for its association with the Beat Generation writers like Jack Kerouac, Allen Ginsberg, and Lawrence Ferlinghetti. City Lights Bookstore is a historic independent bookstore that was a gathering spot for Beat writers and is a must-see for literature lovers.

Cafes, Eateries, and Sights:

Caffè Trieste: Established in 1956, this cafe is a North Beach institution. It's a perfect place to enjoy an authentic Italian espresso or cappuccino while soaking in the old-world charm of the neighborhood.

Scoma's: A classic seafood restaurant situated right on the water with views of the bay, Scoma's serves up fresh, local seafood and is a popular choice for anyone looking to indulge in a quintessential San Francisco dining experience. Don't miss their crab cioppino or clam chowder.

Tony's Pizza Napoletana: If you love pizza, this place is a must. Known for its award-winning Neapolitan pizza, Tony's brings authentic Italian pizza to the heart of North Beach with a wide variety of styles to choose from. It's often hailed as one of the best pizza places in the city.

The Italian Delis and Markets: Wander down Columbus Avenue and explore the family-owned Italian delis and markets, where you can pick up everything from homemade pasta to fresh mozzarella. Molinaris Delicatessen has been around for over 100 years and is a great spot for sandwiches and other Italian specialties.

Nature and Day Trips

San Francisco's stunning natural surroundings offer a wide range of outdoor activities, from towering redwoods and rugged coastlines to peaceful parks and scenic hiking trails. Whether you're a nature lover, an adventurer, or someone looking to unwind in peaceful green spaces, these day trips and outdoor areas around the city offer something for everyone. Here are three top nature spots to explore: Muir Woods, Point Reyes, and Lands End/Golden Gate Park.

Muir Woods:

Muir Woods National Monument is a true sanctuary for those looking to immerse themselves in nature. Nestled just a short drive from San Francisco, this ancient forest is home to some of the tallest trees in the world: the majestic Coastal Redwoods. Walking through Muir Woods feels like stepping back in time, into a quiet, almost magical world where everything slows down, and the towering trees create a cathedral-like atmosphere.

Serene Atmosphere:

- As you stroll along the well-maintained trails, you'll feel the cool, shaded air and hear the sound of birds chirping and leaves rustling. The forest floor is covered with lush ferns and moss, adding to the tranquility of the environment. The silence in the redwoods is soothing, making it a perfect spot for reflection and relaxation.

- The towering redwood trees, which can grow up to 379 feet (115 meters) tall, have a profound effect on visitors. Their sheer size and ancient age—some trees are more than 1,000 years old—create a sense of awe. Standing next to these giants, you can't help but feel small in the best way possible.

Comparison to Other Nature Spots:

While San Francisco has many beautiful parks and outdoor spaces, Muir Woods stands out because it offers a unique, tranquil experience with the redwoods, which aren't found in other parts of the Bay Area. The closest thing to the peace you'll find here is Henry Cowell Redwoods State Park, about 70 miles south of San Francisco, but Muir Woods is far more accessible and much smaller, which makes it a perfect quick escape from the city.

- Other nature spots around the city like Golden Gate Park or Lands End are also gorgeous, but Muir Woods provides a more immersive experience in the ancient beauty of California's redwood forests, with an air of stillness that's hard to find elsewhere.

Point Reyes:

Point Reyes National Seashore is one of the most remarkable and wild places you can visit near San Francisco. Located about an hour and a half north of the city, this coastal park offers dramatic landscapes that vary from rugged cliffs to sandy beaches and rolling hills. With its expansive views of the Pacific Ocean, wildlife, and historic landmarks, Point Reyes is a must-see for any nature lover.

What's Unique About Point Reyes:

- Dramatic Coastal Views: The seashore offers some of the most picturesque views in Northern California. Visitors can take in expansive ocean vistas from various vantage points, like the Point Reyes Lighthouse, perched dramatically on the edge of a cliff. The lighthouse, established in 1870, is an iconic symbol of the area and is surrounded by an incredibly scenic landscape.

- Diverse Ecosystems: Point Reyes is unique because it offers a variety of ecosystems to explore in a relatively small area, from its coastal cliffs to its wetlands, forests, and grassy meadows. You can explore trails that lead through oak woodlands, along the shores of Tomales Bay, or across windswept dunes on Drakes Beach.

- Wildlife Viewing: Point Reyes is a haven for wildlife, including elephant seals, harbor seals, whales, and various bird species. It's an excellent spot for birdwatching, especially in the fall and spring when migratory birds pass through the area. The Tomales Point Trail offers views of migrating animals in their natural habitat.

- Isolated Beauty: Unlike other coastal parks in California, Point Reyes has an isolated charm. It is less commercialized, which makes for a more immersive and unspoiled experience. The park's lack of development allows for a tranquil environment where you can truly connect with nature.

Why You Should Visit:

- If you're looking for a place that combines rugged beauty, diverse wildlife, and peaceful isolation, Point Reyes is ideal. It's perfect for day trips that offer more than just a hike—it's a full-on sensory experience with the sights, sounds, and smells of nature. You can hike to Chimney Rock, visit the Point Reyes Shipwreck, or even check out the Stinson Beach nearby for a more relaxed day by the ocean.

Land End and Golden Gate Park:

Both Land End and Golden Gate Park are large green spaces that provide visitors with a diverse range of experiences, from hiking and wildlife viewing to cultural exploration. They represent the best of San Francisco's ability to blend natural beauty with human-made attractions.

Land End:

- Scenic Hiking: Land End is located at the northwestern edge of San Francisco, where the rugged coastline meets the Pacific Ocean. Its Land End Trail is one of the most scenic hikes in the city, offering stunning views of the Golden Gate Bridge and the Farallon Islands. The trail is an easy-to-moderate hike that takes you along cliffs, through lush cypress trees, and past the old Sutro Baths, a historic site and former swimming complex.

- Ocean Views and Wildlife: As you hike, you'll be treated to panoramic ocean views and the chance to spot wildlife, such as bald eagles, sea lions, and whales (especially during migration season). The beauty and ruggedness of the landscape make this an unforgettable experience.

- Cultural Landmarks: Don't miss the Sutro Heights Park, which was once the private estate of wealthy San Francisco businessman Adolph Sutro, where you can explore the remnants of his garden and enjoy sweeping views of the coast.

Golden Gate Park:

Diverse Attractions: Golden Gate Park, spanning over 1,000 acres, offers something for everyone. Whether you want to take a stroll through lush gardens, visit art museums, or even rent a pedal boat, there's a wide range of experiences within the park's boundaries. The de Young Museum, which features an incredible collection of American art, and the California Academy of Sciences, which houses an aquarium, planetarium, and natural history museum, are two of the park's cultural highlights.

Nature Trails and Gardens: Golden Gate Park also offers extensive green spaces, including the Japanese Tea Garden, where visitors can experience tranquility in a beautiful, traditional Japanese setting. The San Francisco Botanical Garden is another peaceful escape, showcasing over 8,000 different types of plants from around the world.

Active Outdoors: If you're looking for outdoor activities, Golden Gate Park has several opportunities for biking, jogging, and picnicking. The park is also home to Stow Lake, a serene spot for paddle boating or walking around its scenic shores.

Hidden Gems and Local Favorites

San Francisco is a city known for its well-known landmarks, but some of its most unforgettable experiences come from exploring the local gems that aren't always in the guidebooks. These spots offer a blend of relaxation, local flavor, and stunning views, providing a deeper, more intimate connection to the city. Whether you're hanging out with locals or looking for unique places to explore, here are three hidden gems that make San Francisco a truly special place: Dolores Park, Twin Peaks, and Ferry Building Marketplace.

Dolores Park:

Dolores Park is one of the most beloved green spaces in San Francisco, attracting locals and tourists alike with its stunning views, vibrant atmosphere, and prime location. Nestled between the bustling neighborhoods of Mission District and Castro, this park is a hub of social activity and a perfect place to soak in the city's unique vibe.

What Makes Dolores Park a Favorite Hangout Spot for Locals?

- Central Location: Dolores Park is at the heart of one of San Francisco's most vibrant areas, with easy access to both the Mission District's eateries and the Castro's cultural landmarks. Its proximity to local cafes, restaurants, and shops makes it a convenient and popular spot to relax after a day of exploration.
- Sunny, Warm Spot: The park's location and position relative to the surrounding hills make it one of the sunniest places in San Francisco. While much of the city can be foggy and cool, Dolores Park enjoys pleasant, warm weather, particularly on

summer days, which is a rare and appreciated treat.

- Laid-back, Social Atmosphere: Locals flock to Dolores Park to socialize, relax, and enjoy the outdoors. It's a space where you'll see friends lounging on picnic blankets, playing Frisbee, and having impromptu picnics. The lively yet relaxed atmosphere is infectious, and it's a great place to people-watch and immerse yourself in the local culture.

Activities Visitors Can Enjoy:

- Picnics and Sunbathing: Bring your own snacks or grab a bite from one of the nearby cafes and settle into the grass for a relaxing afternoon. It's common to see locals lounging in the sun, reading books, or playing music.

- Tennis and Sports: The park offers tennis courts, basketball courts, and open fields for playing sports, making it an active space for both recreation and leisure. Whether you're playing a casual game of soccer or just watching a match, there's always something fun going on.

- Stunning Views: From the upper part of the park, you can get a spectacular panoramic view of the San Francisco skyline, the Golden Gate Bridge, and Twin Peaks in the distance. It's an excellent spot for photography, especially at sunset when the city lights start to twinkle.

Twin Peaks

Twin Peaks offers one of the most breathtaking and panoramic views of San Francisco, making it a must-visit destination for anyone wanting to take in the beauty of the city from above. This pair of hills stands at 922 feet and offers sweeping vistas of the downtown skyline, the Golden Gate Bridge, Bay Bridge, and beyond.

Best Times to Visit:

- Morning: Visiting Twin Peaks early in the morning offers a serene experience, with fewer crowds and clear, crisp air. You'll get to enjoy the peaceful surroundings and catch some of the best sunrise views of the city. Early mornings are often quieter, giving you a chance to take in the sights without distractions.

- Late Afternoon/Early Evening: Late afternoon and early evening are also great times to visit, as you'll see the city bathed in the warm glow of the golden hour. As the sun begins to set, the colors of the sky and the lights of the city come alive, offering one of the best sunset spots in San Francisco. The changing light creates a magical, almost cinematic atmosphere.

- Nighttime: If you're interested in night photography or simply want to enjoy a peaceful, evening view of the illuminated city, Twin Peaks at night is incredible. The skyline of downtown San Francisco, with the lights sparkling below, is a stunning sight, and the quiet at night adds to the tranquil experience.

What Can Travelers Expect:

- Panoramic Views: From the summit of Twin Peaks, you'll be treated to an unparalleled, 360-degree view of San Francisco and the surrounding area. This is one of the best places to get a bird's-eye view of the Golden Gate Bridge, the Bay Area, and other iconic landmarks like Alcatraz Island.

- Hiking Opportunities: If you're up for a bit of a hike, there are trails around Twin Peaks that take you through serene hillside areas. These trails allow visitors to explore nature while enjoying spectacular views of the city. The area around Twin Peaks is more peaceful and less touristy, making it a great escape from the hustle and bustle of San Francisco.

- Quiet Serenity: While Twin Peaks is a popular spot for tourists, it still feels like a hidden gem compared to other high-traffic viewing spots in the city. It's quiet and tranquil, making it a perfect place to take a moment of solitude, reflect, or simply enjoy the peaceful scenery.

Ferry Building Marketplace:

The Ferry Building Marketplace is a food lover's dream come true. Located on the San Francisco waterfront, the Ferry Building is not only a transit hub for ferries but also home to one of the best artisanal food markets in the country. It brings together the finest local producers, food artisans, and gourmet vendors, making it a must-visit for anyone interested in tasting the best of what California has to offer.

Why Ferry Building is a Food Lover's Haven:

- Local Producers and Artisanal Goods: The Ferry Building features a wide range of local food producers, from artisan cheeses to fresh seafood, organic produce, and even locally roasted coffee. You'll find everything from handmade chocolates to freshly baked bread, and many of these artisanal shops focus on quality, sustainability, and locally sourced ingredients.

- Iconic Vendors: Some must-try spots inside the marketplace include:
  - Cowgirl Creamery: Known for their rich, flavorful cheeses, Cowgirl Creamery offers artisanal, locally made cheese, including the famous Mt. Tam.
  - Ferry Plaza Farmers Market: Open on Tuesdays, Thursdays, and Saturdays, this market is a gathering of top local farmers and vendors offering fresh produce, artisanal goods, and prepared meals.
  - Blue Bottle Coffee: A local favorite for coffee aficionados, Blue Bottle serves up freshly brewed coffee from a minimalist, yet inviting space within the Ferry Building. Don't forget to try one of their hand-poured espressos or seasonal pastries.
  - Hog Island Oyster Co.: If you're a seafood lover, Hog Island is a must-visit. Enjoy fresh oysters shucked right in front of you, or indulge in their clam chowder for a true San Francisco seafood experience.

Must-Try Items:

- Acme Bread: Known for their freshly baked sourdough, Acme Bread is a local institution. Their loaves are made with organic, locally sourced flour and have a distinct San Francisco flavor.

- Roli Roti: A famous rotisserie chicken vendor offering tender, juicy chicken roasted to perfection with a crispy skin. Their porchetta (roast pork) is also a fan favorite.

- Miette Patisserie: A charming bakery serving gourmet pastries, including macarons, cakes, and tarts. Their sweets are visually stunning and absolutely delicious.

Why You Should Visit: The Ferry Building Marketplace is a hub for food culture in San Francisco, with an emphasis on sustainability, local produce, and craftsmanship. Whether you're picking up artisan cheeses, enjoying a meal with a view of the Bay Bridge, or grabbing a quick bite to go, the marketplace provides an unmatched opportunity to sample the best flavors from around California. It's the perfect spot to spend a few hours immersing yourself in the local food scene, and it's a great way to take a break while exploring the waterfront.

Cultural and Artistic Hotspots

Los Angeles is a city known for its vibrant arts scene, and its cultural and artistic hotspots are a must-visit for anyone wanting to dive deeper into the world of art, history, and architecture. Two of the city's most prominent museums—the Getty Center and LACMA—offer world-class collections, stunning architecture, and beautiful gardens that provide visitors with an unforgettable experience. Here's an in-depth look at what makes each of these spots an essential part of your LA adventure:

The Getty Center.

The Getty Center is a spectacular museum that combines exceptional art collections with breathtaking architecture and meticulously curated gardens, all set against a stunning backdrop of the Santa Monica Mountains. Located in the hills of West Los Angeles, this museum offers not just art but an immersive experience that engages all the senses.

Art and Architecture:

- Architectural Masterpiece: Designed by architect Richard Meier, the Getty Center is a modern architectural gem. The museum's white travertine stone buildings and geometric structures create a clean, minimalist look that contrasts beautifully with the surrounding landscape. The museum's design makes the most of its location, with panoramic views of LA, creating an artistic experience that is as much about the space itself as the art it houses.

- Innovative Layout: The Getty Center's layout is designed to lead visitors on an engaging journey through the collection. Its unique central plaza is surrounded by the museum's wings, and visitors can easily navigate between art galleries, the garden, and the research center, ensuring a flow that offers both discovery and reflection.

Gardens:

- The Central Garden at the Getty Center is a living work of art in itself. Designed by artist Robert Irwin, it is a dynamic landscape that changes with the seasons. The garden features a maze-like network of walkways, water features, and a reflecting pool that serves as a focal point for the museum. The flower beds and seasonal plantings are designed to provide color throughout the year, making this garden a peaceful retreat for visitors who want to relax and enjoy the surrounding beauty.

- One of the most striking features of the garden is the Tree Garden, which showcases a variety of species, including California native plants and Mediterranean plants, that beautifully reflect the local ecosystem.

World-Class Collections:

- The Getty Center is renowned for its art collections, which span over 1,000 years of history. Visitors can explore collections that include European paintings, sculpture, decorative arts, and manuscripts, with pieces by famous artists such as Rembrandt, Van Gogh, Turner, and Monet. The Getty Museum also houses a remarkable collection of Greek and Roman antiquities, European decorative arts, and an impressive photography collection.

- Special exhibitions at the Getty are regularly updated, and past exhibitions have included topics ranging from Ancient Egypt to Contemporary Art, ensuring there's always something fresh to see. The museum offers a perfect blend of historical art and cutting-edge exhibitions, making it a vital stop for art lovers of all tastes.

Why You Should Visit: The Getty Center is more than just an art museum—it's an entire sensory experience. The combination of world-class art, beautiful gardens, and breathtaking architecture makes it a must-visit for anyone in Los Angeles. With its stunning views, peaceful gardens, and inspiring collections, it's the perfect spot to spend an afternoon immersed in culture, history, and beauty.

LACMA (Los Angeles County Museum of Art).

As one of the largest and most prestigious art museums in the United States, LACMA (the Los Angeles County Museum of Art) offers an unparalleled collection that spans 6,000 years of art history, making it an essential stop for anyone interested in exploring diverse artistic traditions. Located in the heart of Los Angeles, LACMA is a museum that not only showcases a remarkable variety of art collections, but also hosts groundbreaking special exhibitions, film screenings, and cultural events.

Artistic Diversity:

- LACMA is home to an extensive collection that represents global art from ancient times to the present. It's one of the few museums that offers an impressive range of American, Latin American, Asian, European, and Islamic art, alongside contemporary works. From ancient Chinese bronzes to Native American art, from European masterpieces to modern installations, LACMA's collection reflects the diversity of global culture.

- Some of the must-see highlights of the collection include works by Picasso, Cézanne, and Monet, as well as the California art collection, which explores the state's rich artistic history. The museum also houses an important collection of Mexican and Latin American art, featuring works by artists like Diego Rivera and Frida Kahlo.

Iconic Exhibits and Architecture:

- Chris Burden's "Urban Light": One of LACMA's most famous installations is Chris Burden's "Urban Light", an outdoor sculpture made up of 202 restored street lamps. It has become an iconic sight in Los Angeles, and visitors flock to take photos at this captivating installation, especially at night when the lamps are illuminated.
- The Resnick Pavilion: LACMA's Resnick Pavilion features a spacious, modern design and regularly hosts special exhibitions that highlight the works of both established and emerging artists. The building itself is a remarkable feat of architecture, designed by Renzo Piano, and provides the perfect setting for contemporary art displays.

Special Events and Programs:

- Special Exhibitions: LACMA is known for its innovative exhibitions that cover a wide range of topics—from contemporary art and photography to ancient civilizations. Past exhibitions have included works by artists like David Hockney, James Turrell, and Jeff Koons. The museum also frequently collaborates with other major institutions to bring exclusive collections to LA.

- Film and Music Programs: LACMA regularly hosts film screenings, including special retrospectives, documentaries, and classic films. For those who are fans of cinema, the museum's Film Independent at LACMA program is a great way to explore film culture. LACMA also hosts live music performances, often incorporating sound and art as part of their exhibitions.

- LACMA's Free Programs: On certain days, LACMA offers free admission to specific exhibitions or hosts free programs like art-making workshops, film screenings, and special talks. These are excellent opportunities for visitors to experience world-class art at little to no cost.

Why You Should Visit: LACMA is not just a museum—it's a cultural hub that offers a dynamic, immersive experience. With its impressive collection, cutting-edge exhibitions, and vibrant events, LACMA provides a deeper understanding of global culture, history, and contemporary creativity.

Whether you're an art lover, a history buff, or someone simply curious about the world's artistic heritage, LACMA's diverse collections and programs offer something for everyone. It's the perfect place to immerse yourself in the cultural pulse of Los Angeles.

Top Neighborhoods to Visit

Los Angeles is a sprawling city of contrasts, where vibrant neighborhoods each offer their own unique experiences. From the laid-back, artistic vibe of Venice Beach to the glitz and glamour of Beverly Hills, and the eclectic mix of modern and historic in Downtown LA, each neighborhood provides a different taste of LA's multifaceted character. Here's a deeper look at these top neighborhoods:

Venice Beach.

Venice Beach is one of the most iconic neighborhoods in Los Angeles, known for its eclectic and laid-back atmosphere. Founded in 1905 by millionaire Abbot Kinney, Venice was initially designed as a resort town, but it has since evolved into a vibrant and bohemian district that reflects the creative soul of LA.

What Makes Venice Beach Stand Out:

- Bohemian Vibes: Venice Beach is often considered the heart of LA's counterculture, and the neighborhood thrives on individuality and artistic expression. With its funky boutiques, street art, and colorful murals, Venice feels like an open-air gallery. The Venice Canals, which were inspired by Venice, Italy, provide a more serene side of the neighborhood with charming, waterfront homes.

- The Venice Boardwalk: One of the area's most famous features is the Venice Beach Boardwalk, a lively stretch along the beach where you'll find a mix of street performers, muscle beach bodybuilders, skateboarders, vendors, and artists. It's a great spot to people-watch, shop for unique goods, or enjoy an impromptu performance.

How Visitors Can Take In the Eclectic Mix of Art, Surf, and Fun:

- Explore the Venice Canals: A quieter spot compared to the bustling boardwalk, the Venice Canals are a peaceful escape where visitors can walk along the waterways, watch the ducks, or admire the unique homes lining the canals.

- Venice Beach Skate Park: If you love skateboarding or simply want to see some impressive tricks, head to the Venice Skate

Park, one of the most famous in the world. The park attracts talented skateboarders from around the globe.

- Art Walks and Galleries: Venice is known for its artistic vibe, and the neighborhood is home to various art galleries, street art, and public art installations. First Fridays on Abbot Kinney Boulevard are a popular event where you can enjoy art openings, food trucks, and live music, making it a perfect evening out for both locals and visitors.

- Muscle Beach: Venice Beach is also famous for Muscle Beach, a historic outdoor gym that's been around since the 1930s. Here, bodybuilders and fitness enthusiasts can be seen working out while visitors look on. It's a great place to get a sense of the neighborhood's unique blend of beach culture and physicality.

Beverly Hills.

Beverly Hills is the epitome of luxury and glamour in Los Angeles. Known for its palm-lined streets, high-end shopping, and celebrity residents, Beverly Hills offers visitors a glimpse into the world of the rich and famous.

Best Ways to Explore Beverly Hills:

- Rodeo Drive: Perhaps one of the most famous shopping streets in the world, Rodeo Drive is a must-visit for those looking to indulge in luxury. With designer boutiques like Gucci, Louis Vuitton, and Chanel, it's a shopper's paradise. Even if you're not planning on splurging, it's fun to stroll down the street, window shop, and possibly spot a celebrity.

- Beverly Gardens Park: This historic park is one of the most beautiful green spaces in the area, providing a scenic and peaceful spot for visitors. The Beverly Hills Sign in the park makes for a perfect photo opportunity, with its iconic neon lights at night.

- Celebrity Homes Tour: Beverly Hills is home to some of Hollywood's biggest stars. You can take a guided celebrity homes tour that will take you past the mansions of A-list stars (both past and present). While the homes themselves are private, the tour guides often share insider gossip and fun stories about celebrity lifestyles and history.

- Greystone Mansion and Park: Built in 1928, this grand estate is one of the largest and most historic mansions in Beverly Hills. The mansion is open to the public for tours, and its beautifully landscaped gardens are perfect for a leisurely stroll.

What Makes Beverly Hills Unforgettable:

- High-End Dining and Nightlife: Beverly Hills offers a wealth of fine dining options, many of which are celebrity hotspots. Restaurants like Spago (owned by Wolfgang Puck) and The Grill on the Alley offer gourmet dining experiences, while bars like The Polo Lounge at the Beverly Hills Hotel have long been a favorite hangout for the stars.

- Beverly Hills Trolley Tour: For a quick and informative tour of the area, hop on the Beverly Hills Trolley Tour, which will take you through the beautiful tree-lined streets, past iconic landmarks, and around the gorgeous neighborhoods. You'll learn about the area's history, famous residents, and more.

Downtown LA

Downtown LA (DTLA) is the beating heart of the city, where old and new collide in a dynamic urban environment. From sleek, modern skyscrapers to historic landmarks, DTLA offers a fascinating mix of culture, history, and cutting-edge creativity that reflects the diversity and energy of Los Angeles.

The Essence of Downtown LA:

- **Modern Attractions and Landmarks:** DTLA is home to some of the city's most important modern landmarks, such as the Walt Disney Concert Hall designed by Frank Gehry, and The Broad, a contemporary art museum with an impressive collection of modern works. Grand Park provides an open space for both relaxation and events, offering stunning views of city landmarks like City Hall.

- **Historic Buildings:** In addition to its modern attractions, DTLA is rich in history. Olvera Street, the birthplace of Los Angeles, is a bustling market and cultural center that gives visitors a sense of the city's Spanish roots. The Bradbury Building, with its ornate Victorian-era architecture, is another iconic historic building that showcases LA's unique design legacy.

- **Cultural Energy:** Downtown LA is an artistic hub, where you can experience live theater at The Theatre at Ace Hotel, explore murals in the Arts District, or catch a live performance at the Walt Disney Concert Hall. It's also a place where tech culture, street art, and creative industries come together, making it a melting pot of cultures and styles.

What to Do in Downtown LA:

- **Explore the Arts District:** This neighborhood is filled with street art, galleries, and hipster cafes. The Art Walk is a popular monthly event, where visitors can explore local galleries and sample food from food trucks that line the streets.

- Visit the Grand Central Market: One of the oldest landmarks in DTLA, the Grand Central Market is a food lover's haven with a wide array of local vendors, from gourmet tacos to fresh produce and homemade ice cream. It's a great place to sample LA's diverse food scene.

- The Last Bookstore: A visit to DTLA wouldn't be complete without stopping by The Last Bookstore, one of the largest and most unique independent bookstores in the country. It's a beloved spot for both book lovers and Instagrammers, thanks to its whimsical art installations and extensive collection of books.

- Skyscraper Views: DTLA is also home to The US Bank Tower, the tallest building in California, which offers 360-degree views of the city. From its observation deck, visitors can enjoy panoramic views of the city's sprawling urban landscape.

Why DTLA Captures the City's Energy:

- Diverse Neighborhoods: The area includes a rich mix of diverse neighborhoods, from the artistic vibe of the Arts District to the historic core with its old-world architecture and iconic landmarks. Each area brings its own flavor to the overall essence of DTLA, offering a true snapshot of LA's diverse cultural energy.

- A Hub of Activity: From the downtown skyline to the vibrant nightlife, farmers markets, and street festivals, DTLA is where the pulse of LA can be felt most strongly. Whether you're into art, history, food, or shopping, Downtown LA has a little bit of everything that reflects the city's multifaceted character.

Nature and Day Trips

Los Angeles is surrounded by an abundance of natural beauty, from stunning beaches to scenic hiking trails, making it the perfect gateway for memorable day trips and weekend getaways. Whether you're seeking a peaceful escape along the coast or a city with a rich blend of history and culture, here are three top destinations that will make your LA trip even more rewarding: Malibu, Santa Barbara, and San Diego.

Malibu

Malibu is a coastal paradise known for its stunning beaches, upscale dining, and dramatic scenery. Just a short drive from Los Angeles, this idyllic beach town has been a favorite getaway for celebrities and travelers alike for decades. Its relaxed vibe and picturesque surroundings make it an excellent choice for a beach day, outdoor adventure, or fine dining experience.

What Makes Malibu Alluring:

- Beaches: Malibu's beaches are some of the most beautiful in California, offering everything from surfing to serene sunbathing. Zuma Beach is known for its long, wide shoreline, perfect for families and beachgoers. For a more secluded experience, El Matador Beach (one of Malibu's lesser-known gems) is a stunning spot with sea caves, rocky outcrops, and picturesque views.

- Hiking: Malibu also offers amazing hiking opportunities with sweeping ocean views. The Solstice Canyon Trail is a great moderate hike that takes you through beautiful landscapes and past the ruins of an old ranch house. Point Dume State Beach is another popular spot with trails that lead you to the cliffs overlooking the ocean.

- Upscale Dining: After a day of sun and adventure, indulge in Malibu's fine dining scene. Famous spots like Nobu Malibu offer world-class cuisine with unbeatable views of the ocean. Geoffrey's Malibu provides a classic dining experience overlooking the water, making it a favorite among locals and tourists.

Top Spots to Visit:

- Malibu Pier: A great spot for a leisurely stroll, Malibu Pier offers excellent views of the coastline and is home to several casual eateries, including Malibu Farm.

- The Getty Villa: Located just off the Pacific Coast Highway, The Getty Villa is an art museum set in a beautiful Roman-inspired villa overlooking the Pacific. It's perfect for history and art lovers, with collections of ancient Greek and Roman antiquities.

- Point Dume State Beach: Known for its stunning vistas, this is an ideal spot for a picnic, a hike, or a relaxing afternoon in the sun.

Santa Barbara

Just a two-hour drive up the coast from Los Angeles, Santa Barbara offers a charming escape from the hustle and bustle of the city. Known as the "American Riviera," Santa Barbara boasts beautiful beaches, Spanish colonial architecture, and a laid-back atmosphere that makes it an ideal weekend getaway or day trip.

Why Visit Santa Barbara:

- Scenic Beauty: Santa Barbara sits at the foot of the Santa Ynez Mountains, offering stunning views of the ocean and mountains. The combination of palm-lined beaches and mediterranean-style architecture creates a picture-perfect setting that's easy to fall in love with.

- Wineries: The area is also home to some of California's best wineries. Santa Barbara is located within the renowned Santa Ynez Valley, where you can enjoy a wine tour and tastings at world-class wineries such as Sunstone Vineyards and Foxen Winery.

- Santa Barbara's Historic Mission: Founded in 1786, the Mission Santa Barbara is one of the most stunning and well-preserved missions in California. Visitors can learn about the history of the area and admire the architecture and gardens of the mission.

Top Spots to Visit:

- State Street: Known for its charming atmosphere, State Street is lined with shops, cafes, restaurants, and art galleries. It's a perfect place to walk, shop, and grab a bite to eat.

- Stearns Wharf: This historic pier offers a great view of the coastline and is home to restaurants, a marine center, and some fantastic spots for seafood and souvenirs.

- Santa Barbara Botanic Garden: For nature lovers, this botanical garden showcases the native plants of California, offering a serene place to explore and learn about the region's flora.

San Diego

San Diego is located just a two-hour drive south of Los Angeles and offers a fantastic variety of attractions, from its famous zoo to its gorgeous beaches and vibrant cultural scene. While LA is known for its entertainment and glamour, San Diego's laid-back atmosphere and family-friendly vibe make it a perfect complement to your LA visit.

What Makes San Diego Great:

- Beaches: San Diego is home to some of the most beautiful beaches in California. Whether you're into surfing at Pacific Beach, relaxing at Coronado Beach, or enjoying the family-friendly atmosphere at La Jolla Cove, there's a beach for every taste.

- San Diego Zoo: The San Diego Zoo, located in Balboa Park, is one of the most famous zoos in the world. It's home to over 3,500 animals across hundreds of species, including giant pandas, koalas, and polar bears. With its lush landscapes and expansive exhibits, it's a must-visit for animal lovers of all ages.

- Cultural Attractions: Balboa Park is not only home to the zoo but also to numerous museums, gardens, and performing arts venues. Visitors can explore the San Diego Museum of Art, The Old Globe Theatre, and Botanical Building, all set in the park's gorgeous surroundings.

Top Spots to Visit:

- Old Town San Diego: A historic district with vibrant markets, shops, and museums that showcase San Diego's Mexican heritage. It's a great place for lunch and to pick up local goods.

- Gaslamp Quarter: The Gaslamp Quarter offers a taste of San Diego's nightlife, with its Victorian-style buildings housing trendy bars, restaurants, and nightclubs. It's the perfect place to go for dinner and drinks.

- USS Midway Museum: This historic aircraft carrier is now a museum where visitors can learn about naval history and explore the ship's deck and aircrafts.

Local Tips and Hidden Spots

Los Angeles is a city full of well-known landmarks and famous attractions, but it also has plenty of hidden gems that allow visitors to experience a different, more unique side of the city. Whether you're looking for a peaceful beach, a quirky bookstore, or a chance to capture one of LA's most iconic images, these local spots are perfect for those who want to go beyond the ordinary.

El Matador Beach

El Matador Beach is one of Malibu's hidden treasures, tucked away between the more popular Zuma Beach and Point Dume. Unlike Malibu's other beaches, which can get crowded, El Matador offers a peaceful, secluded atmosphere with stunning views and rocky cliffs.

Why It's a Hidden Gem:

- Seclusion: With limited parking and a short walk down a steep path, El Matador isn't as easy to access as some of Malibu's more famous beaches. This means it's often less crowded, giving visitors a quiet place to relax and enjoy the natural beauty of the coastline.

- Scenic Beauty: The beach is known for its dramatic sea stacks and rock formations that rise out of the water, providing fantastic photo opportunities, especially at sunset.

- Peaceful Vibe: El Matador Beach is perfect for those looking to get away from the hustle and bustle. Visitors can take a peaceful walk along the shore, have a picnic, or just sit and enjoy the sound of the waves crashing against the rocks.

The Last Bookstore

The Last Bookstore in downtown Los Angeles is a quirky, multi-level bookstore that has become a must-visit for bibliophiles and Instagrammers. Known for its eclectic vibe, creative book displays, and extensive collection of both new and used books, it's a place where visitors can lose themselves in stories and art.

Why You Should Visit:

- Unique Book Displays: The store features eye-catching displays like bookshelves turned into art installations, and the "book tunnel" made entirely of old books, which is one of the most photographed spots in the city.

- Artistic Atmosphere: The Last Bookstore isn't just about buying books; it's a space for art, creativity, and inspiration. You can find local art, vinyl records, and even vintage collectibles as you explore the store.

- Instagram-Worthy: For those looking for the perfect shot, the bookstore is a treasure trove of photo opportunities. Whether you're posing in front of the book tunnel or sitting in one of the cozy corners, it's a place where every angle is a potential Instagram post.

LACMA's Urban Light

LACMA's Urban Light installation by artist Chris Burden is one of Los Angeles' most iconic sights. The installation consists of 202 restored lampposts from the 1920s, arranged in a grid-like pattern in front of the LACMA museum. The sight of the lights lit up at night is a quintessential LA experience.

How to Capture the Lights:

- Golden Hour and Night Shots: For unique shots, visit during golden hour just before sunset, when the warm light of the setting sun reflects off the lamps. Alternatively, nighttime shots are equally mesmerizing, as the lights illuminate the urban landscape in a magical glow.

- Perspective: Experiment with different angles and perspectives. Wide-angle shots can capture the full scope of the installation, while close-ups of individual lights against the dark night sky can offer a dramatic effect.

- Family or Group Shots: Urban Light is a popular spot for family photos, couples, and groups. Its symmetry and bright lights make it a fun and memorable place to capture special moments.

Part III: Travel Preparation Guide.

Getting There

The best flight options to both cities

Top airlines and tips for finding deals.

When flying into San Francisco or Los Angeles, there are several airlines offering direct flights, making it convenient for travelers. Both cities are major hubs with excellent international and domestic connectivity.

For San Francisco (SFO): Airlines like United Airlines, American Airlines, Delta Air Lines, and Alaska Airlines offer direct flights from major cities worldwide. If you're flying internationally, Singapore Airlines and Lufthansa provide comfortable connections. Look for flights on budget carriers like JetBlue or Southwest Airlines for cheaper options.

For Los Angeles (LAX): American Airlines, Delta Air Lines, Alaska Airlines, and United Airlines dominate the routes to LAX, with multiple daily direct flights from both domestic and international locations. Norwegian Air and WOW Air are great low-cost international options from Europe.

Tips for Finding Deals:

Book in Advance: To find the best deals, try to book at least 2-3 months ahead of your trip.

Use Price Comparison Sites: Websites like Google Flights, Skyscanner, and Kayak help you compare airfares and track prices.

Set Fare Alerts: Set price alerts on these sites to get notified when prices drop for your preferred routes.

How do travelers get from the airport to the main areas of the cities? Should they use a shuttle, taxi, or public transit?

San Francisco:

From SFO, the BART (Bay Area Rapid Transit) system is a fast and affordable option to get to downtown San Francisco. It takes about 30 minutes and costs around $9.

Taxis or ride-sharing services like Uber or Lyft are convenient but more expensive, costing about $40–$60 depending on your destination in the city.

Airport Shuttles are available, but they might take longer as they make stops at multiple locations.

Los Angeles:

From LAX, the FlyAway Bus is a good choice for getting to various parts of LA, like Santa Monica or Union Station, for about $9–$12.

Taxis and ride-sharing services are available but may be costly during rush hour, ranging from $40 to $70, depending on the traffic and destination.

Public Transit (Metro) can take longer but is budget-friendly. You can use the C Line from LAX to get to downtown LA.

Transportation Within the Cities

Discuss public transport options (BART in San Francisco, Metro in LA) and how to use them effectively.

San Francisco (BART)

The BART (Bay Area Rapid Transit) system is the primary mode of public transport in San Francisco, connecting key areas like downtown, SFO, and Berkeley. The BART is very efficient and is a great way to travel between neighborhoods or get to/from the airport.

How to Use BART: You can buy a Clipper Card (which can be used on BART, buses, and ferries) at the station or use contactless payment with a credit card. BART trains run frequently and have clear routes and schedules. It's cheap, quick, and reliable.

Los Angeles (Metro)

The Metro Rail system in LA connects popular areas like Hollywood, downtown LA, and Santa Monica. The Metro system is especially useful for getting around downtown, Hollywood, and the Wilshire corridor.

How to Use the Metro: You can purchase a TAP card for $2, which is used to board both buses and trains. The trains are clean and convenient, with frequent stops. Be sure to check the schedule and plan ahead as some lines don't run as late as others.

Metro Bus: The Metro Bus is another way to get around the city. It's cheaper than the Metro Rail but can be slower due to traffic.

What are the pros and cons of renting a car in each city, and which one is better suited for tourists looking to drive?

San Francisco:

Pros: Renting a car in San Francisco can be useful if you plan to visit areas outside the city like Muir Woods, Sausalito, or Point Reyes. It offers flexibility for day trips.

Cons: Driving in the city itself can be challenging due to narrow streets, hills, traffic, and expensive parking (some areas charge upwards of $40 per day). Plus, the city's public transport system (BART) is efficient and can take you to most places.

Recommendation: It's generally easier to avoid renting a car in San Francisco unless you plan to venture beyond the city. Public transport and ride-sharing services like Uber are great alternatives.

Los Angeles:

Pros: Renting a car in LA is almost a necessity if you want to explore the city at your own pace. With sprawling neighborhoods, a car is ideal for exploring areas like Santa Monica, Venice Beach, and Beverly Hills. The city is known for its freeways, and driving gives you flexibility.

Cons: Traffic is a major downside of driving in LA, especially during rush hours. Finding parking in popular areas like Hollywood or downtown can be difficult and expensive. Plus, LA's public transit system isn't as extensive as other cities.

Recommendation: If you're comfortable with driving, renting a car is often the best option in LA, especially for visiting neighborhoods that are far from each other. Just be prepared for traffic and high parking fees.

Accommodations

When traveling to San Francisco and Los Angeles, choosing the right neighborhood to stay in can significantly enhance your experience. Both cities offer a wide range of accommodation options, from luxury hotels to affordable hostels and vacation rentals, catering to families, solo adventurers, and couples. Here's a breakdown of the best neighborhoods to stay in, plus insights into the benefits of different types of accommodations.

San Francisco: Recommended Neighborhoods to Stay In

1. For Families: Fisherman's Wharf

Why Stay Here: Fisherman's Wharf is a family-friendly area with a ton of attractions nearby, including Pier 39, Aquarium of the Bay, and Ghirardelli Square. It's also very close to Alcatraz Island and Golden Gate Bridge, making it convenient for sightseeing. The area has plenty of family-oriented hotels, restaurants, and activities.

Address: Fisherman's Wharf, San Francisco, CA 94133

Recommended Accommodation: Hotel Zephyr – A playful, family-friendly hotel with a great location right by the waterfront.

2. For Solo Adventurers: Mission District

Why Stay Here: The Mission District is vibrant, with lots of street art, lively cafes, and affordable dining options. It's a culturally rich neighborhood known for its hip atmosphere, making it a popular choice for solo travelers looking to explore local art, food, and nightlife. It's also centrally located, allowing easy access to other parts of the city.

Address: Mission District, San Francisco, CA

Recommended Accommodation: The Mission Inn – A budget-friendly boutique hotel, offering simple, comfortable rooms with a modern touch.

3. For Couples: Nob Hill

Why Stay Here: Nob Hill is a charming, upscale neighborhood offering panoramic views of the city. It's romantic with its old-world architecture, elegant hotels, and proximity to cultural spots like the Grace Cathedral and the Cable Car Museum. The serene atmosphere makes it an excellent choice for couples.

Address: Nob Hill, San Francisco, CA 94109

Recommended Accommodation: The Fairmont San Francisco – A luxury hotel with stunning views, historic charm, and exceptional service, perfect for a romantic getaway.

Los Angeles: Recommended Neighborhoods to Stay In

1. For Families: Santa Monica

Why Stay Here: Santa Monica is perfect for families due to its beautiful beaches, the iconic Santa Monica Pier, and easy access to attractions like the California Science Center and Venice Beach. It's a more relaxed area with a walkable boardwalk, parks, and family-friendly restaurants, making it a great base for exploring LA.

Address: Santa Monica, CA 90401

Recommended Accommodation: Shore Hotel – A modern, eco-friendly hotel with a family-friendly atmosphere and fantastic beach views.

2. For Solo Adventurers: Downtown LA

Why Stay Here: Downtown LA offers a mix of cultural attractions, artsy vibes, and diverse dining options, perfect for solo travelers. From the Broad Museum to Grand Central Market, there's something for everyone. It's also an excellent base for exploring other parts of the city, with great public transit access.

Address: Downtown Los Angeles, CA 90013

Recommended Accommodation: The Ace Hotel – A trendy spot with an artistic atmosphere, rooftop bar, and close proximity to downtown attractions.

3. For Couples: West Hollywood

Why Stay Here: West Hollywood is known for its lively nightlife, trendy restaurants, and celebrity culture, making it ideal for couples seeking romance and excitement. You can visit places like the Sunset Strip and The Grove, or enjoy intimate dinners in the area's chic dining spots.

Address: West Hollywood, CA 90069

Recommended Accommodation: The London West Hollywood – A luxury hotel that offers stunning views of the city, an incredible rooftop pool, and proximity to great nightlife.

Hotels vs. Vacation Rentals vs. Hostels

When it comes to choosing where to stay in San Francisco or Los Angeles, it's essential to consider your budget, comfort preferences, and the type of experience you want. Here's a quick breakdown of the benefits and drawbacks of each type of accommodation:

Hotels:

Pros:

Comfort and Convenience: Hotels offer a high level of service, including daily housekeeping, room service, and concierge services. They are often centrally located, close to popular attractions, and have amenities like pools, gyms, and restaurants.

Predictable Quality: With well-known hotel chains, you know what you're getting in terms of amenities and service.

Security: Hotels generally offer more security with 24-hour front desk services, key card access, and in-house staff.

Cons:

Cost: Hotels, especially in areas like downtown LA or Fisherman's Wharf, can be expensive, especially if you're booking last minute.

Less Personalization: Hotels can feel more impersonal compared to vacation rentals, where you can enjoy a more local, homely atmosphere.

Vacation Rentals:

Pros:

More Space: Vacation rentals often offer more space than hotels, which is ideal for families or travelers looking for a more home-like atmosphere. You'll have access to kitchens, living rooms, and sometimes even private pools or outdoor areas.

Cost-Effective for Groups: Renting an entire house or apartment can often be more cost-effective for groups or families compared to booking multiple hotel rooms.

Local Experience: Staying in a neighborhood-focused rental can provide a more immersive experience, allowing you to live like a local and explore hidden gems in the city.

Cons:

Inconsistent Quality: The quality of vacation rentals can vary greatly, depending on the host and property. It's essential to read reviews and choose reputable platforms like Airbnb or Vrbo.

Limited Services: Vacation rentals don't offer hotel services like daily cleaning or concierge support. You're on your own when it comes to things like supplies or assistance.

Hostels:

Pros:

Affordable: Hostels are generally the most budget-friendly option, especially for solo travelers or backpackers looking to save on accommodation costs.

Social Atmosphere: Hostels offer a great opportunity to meet other travelers through communal spaces, tours, and activities. This can be ideal for solo adventurers.

Flexible Options: Many hostels offer a range of room types, from dormitories to private rooms, making them adaptable to different budgets.

Cons:

Less Privacy: In dormitory-style rooms, you'll likely share space with other travelers, which can be less comfortable for those who prefer privacy or quiet.

Basic Amenities: Hostels typically offer fewer amenities than hotels or vacation rentals, with shared bathrooms and kitchen facilities.

Packing Essentials

When visiting San Francisco and Los Angeles, it's important to pack for each city's unique climate and the range of temperatures you might encounter. Here's a packing list that prepares you for both the foggy coolness of San Francisco and the sunny warmth of Los Angeles.

San Francisco: San Francisco is known for its foggy, unpredictable weather, so layering is key.

- Light jacket or sweater: San Francisco's weather can change quickly, and it's often chilly, especially near the coast and in the evenings. A windbreaker or light sweater is a must.

- Comfortable walking shoes: San Francisco has many steep hills, so comfortable shoes are essential for exploring the city on foot.

- Layers: Pack t-shirts, long sleeves, and a sweater to layer as the weather shifts. You'll want to be able to adjust depending on the temperature.

- Scarf or shawl: Great for the chillier days or evenings, especially when the fog rolls in.

- Sunglasses: Although foggy weather is common, there are plenty of sunny moments as well, so a good pair of sunglasses will be useful.

Los Angeles: LA is known for its sunny weather, but temperatures can vary by area, so be prepared for both warm days and cooler evenings.

- Light clothing for daytime: Pack shorts, dresses, t-shirts, and tank tops for the warm daytime temperatures, especially if you're spending time near the beaches or in downtown LA.
- Sweater or light jacket: Nights and evenings in LA can cool down quickly, especially if you're near the coast, so have something light to wear.
- Sunscreen: LA's sun can be intense, so be sure to pack sunscreen and reapply regularly to avoid sunburn.
- Swimwear: Don't forget your swimsuit if you plan to spend time at Santa Monica, Venice Beach, or any of the city's pools.
- Comfortable walking shoes: Whether you're exploring LA's neighborhoods, hiking in Griffith Park, or strolling down Rodeo Drive, comfortable shoes are essential.

How to Prepare for the Range of Temperatures:

- Layering is key for both cities. San Francisco can be cold in the morning and evening, while LA may be hot during the day but cool in the evenings, especially in coastal areas.

- Check the weather forecast before your trip to know what to expect on the days you'll be there. Both cities can be unpredictable, so it's best to be prepared for a range of temperatures.

Health, Safety, and Travel Tips

Staying Safe in Crowded Tourist Spots:

- Be aware of your surroundings: Major tourist areas like Fisherman's Wharf in San Francisco or Hollywood Boulevard in LA can get crowded, so it's important to keep an eye on your belongings and be cautious of pickpockets.
- Avoid leaving valuables unattended: Never leave your purse, phone, or other valuables on tables or benches, especially in crowded places.
- Trust your instincts: If something doesn't feel right, it's always better to move to a more populated area or seek help from authorities or local staff.

Avoiding Common Scams:

- Street Performers and "Free Gifts": In places like Venice Beach or Union Square, be wary of street performers or individuals offering "free gifts" or "good luck charms." Often, they'll demand money after giving you something.

- Taxi Scams: In both cities, use ride-sharing apps like Uber or Lyft instead of hailing taxis off the street. If you must take a taxi, ensure it's a licensed one.

- Timeshare Scams: Be cautious of "free tour" offers that are disguised as timeshare promotions. Stick to trusted tourist information sources.

Keeping Belongings Secure:

- Use a money belt or anti-theft backpack: If you're worried about pickpockets, especially in busy areas, use a money belt or a backpack with anti-theft features such as lockable zippers.

- Keep your phone in your pocket: Avoid walking around with your phone out in busy areas like Hollywood or Chinatown. Keep it secured in a zipped pocket.

- Lock up valuables in hotel safes: Most hotels offer safes in rooms for securing important documents, electronics, and money.

Cultural Differences:

- Tipping: Tipping is a standard practice in both cities. In restaurants, 15-20% of the bill is the usual tip for good service. If you're at a bar, $1–$2 per drink is appropriate. Tipping is also expected for taxis, ride-sharing drivers, and hotel staff (around $1–$2 per bag).

- Personal Space: While San Francisco and Los Angeles are generally laid-back cities, personal space is still important. Respect others' space in public transportation, and avoid speaking too loudly or intrusively, especially in quieter areas like cafes or libraries.

- Dress Codes: LA tends to have a relaxed, casual dress code, especially in places like Venice Beach and Santa Monica, but San Francisco may have a more eclectic fashion vibe, particularly in neighborhoods like Mission District or Haight-Ashbury.

Travel Apps and Resources

When navigating a city as large and diverse as Los Angeles or San Francisco, using a few key apps can make your trip smoother, more enjoyable, and less stressful. Here are some essential apps and websites to have on hand:

Essential Apps for Navigating the Cities:

- Google Maps: For navigating both cities, Google Maps is a must-have. It offers directions for walking, driving, and public transport and can help you find nearby attractions, restaurants, and shops.

- Transit (for SF): The Transit app is great for getting around San Francisco via Muni or BART. It provides real-time public transit info, including bus schedules and train routes.

- Metro Los Angeles (for LA): The Metro LA app helps you navigate LA's Metro Rail system and bus routes efficiently.

- Uber/Lyft: For getting around the city without a car, Uber and Lyft are the most reliable and cost-effective options. Both are available in both San Francisco and Los Angeles, and you can easily book a ride via their apps.

- OpenTable: If you're looking for a place to dine, OpenTable lets you make reservations at top restaurants in both cities. It's especially helpful for booking in popular spots like Nobu Malibu or The Slanted Door in San Francisco.

- GrubHub/Postmates: For food delivery, GrubHub and Postmates let you order from a wide variety of restaurants in both cities. Great for days when you don't want to leave the hotel or apartment.

Useful Websites for Local Events and Festivals:

- Time Out Los Angeles: For discovering events, festivals, and nightlife in LA, the Time Out website is a great resource. It lists everything from food festivals to art exhibitions and live music.

- SF Funcheap: For San Francisco, SF Funcheap lists free and low-cost events happening in the city, from outdoor movie nights to pop-up food festivals.

- Eventbrite: For both cities, Eventbrite is a great platform to check for concerts, art shows, food tastings, and more. You can filter by dates, locations, and categories of interest.

Conclusion

With the right preparation, navigating San Francisco and Los Angeles can be a breeze. Packing layers for San Francisco's cool, foggy weather and lighter clothing for LA's sunny climate ensures you're prepared for both cities' diverse conditions. Staying safe by using common sense and keeping your belongings secure will help you avoid mishaps. And with the right apps, you'll be able to explore the cities with ease, whether you're hopping on public transit or finding your next event. Enjoy your trip and soak in all the incredible experiences these cities have to offer!

Part IV: Food & Dining

Food & Dining

San Francisco and Los Angeles are both culinary meccas, offering a diverse range of delicious foods and unique dining experiences. Whether you're indulging in iconic sourdough bread in San Francisco or savoring tacos in LA, these cities are filled with flavors you won't want to miss. Here's a deep dive into must-try foods, hidden gems, and dining tips for your trip!

Must-Try Foods in San Francisco

San Francisco's food scene is a blend of historic flavors, local produce, and fresh seafood. Here are some iconic dishes and hidden gems for food lovers:

Iconic Dishes:

- Sourdough Bread: San Francisco is famous for its sourdough bread, made with a unique starter culture. You can't visit without trying a loaf or a sandwich.

Where to Try: Boudin Bakery at Fisherman's Wharf (Address: 160 Jefferson St, San Francisco, CA 94133). It's a historic bakery known for its classic sourdough bread and delicious clam chowder served in a sourdough bowl.

Seafood at Fisherman's Wharf: The seafood in San Francisco is exceptional, with clam chowder, crab, and other fresh offerings being the star of the show.

- Where to Try: Alioto's Restaurant (Address: 8 Fishermans Wharf, San Francisco, CA 94133). Enjoy fresh crab, clam chowder, and more at this historic waterfront spot.

Mission-Style Burrito: San Francisco is home to the mission-style burrito, a massive wrap filled with rice, beans, meat, and other ingredients, often served foil-wrapped for convenience.

Where to Try: La Taqueria (Address: 2889 Mission St, San Francisco, CA 94110). Known for its delicious carne asada burritos.

Hidden Gems for Great Food Experiences:

- Golden Gate Park Food Trucks: Head to Golden Gate Park for a variety of food trucks offering everything from gourmet burgers to fusion tacos. It's a great place to explore local vendors and sample different cuisines.

Where to Try: Find food trucks near the Park's Music Concourse and Polo Fields.

Ferry Building Marketplace: A fantastic destination for local, artisanal foods. You'll find everything from fresh cheeses to gourmet chocolates, plus a variety of small restaurants and eateries.

Where to Try: Ferry Building Marketplace (Address: 1 Ferry Building, San Francisco, CA 94111). Visit

Cowgirl Creamery for artisan cheeses and Blue Bottle Coffee for an excellent cup of coffee.

- Swan Oyster Depot: An old-school seafood spot known for its fresh oysters, crab, and clam chowder. It's a local favorite with a no-frills, counter service setup.

Where to Try: Swan Oyster Depot (Address: 1517 Polk St, San Francisco, CA 94109).

Must-Try Foods in Los Angeles

Los Angeles is a food paradise, with a blend of ethnic flavors, street food, and innovative dining. Here's a rundown of the best culinary experiences unique to LA:

Must-Try Foods:

- Tacos: Los Angeles is the taco capital of the U.S., and you'll find taco trucks and restaurants serving delicious tacos filled with everything from carnitas to fish.

Where to Try: Guisados (Address: 2100 E 7th St, Los Angeles, CA 90021). Known for their braised meat tacos in unique flavors.

Where to Try: Leo's Taco Truck (Address: South Central LA, 1st Street). This famous food truck serves al pastor tacos with fresh pineapple and marinated pork.

- Korean BBQ: LA has a huge Korean population, making it the perfect city to experience the tradition of Korean BBQ. Grilled meats, kimchi, and banchan (side dishes) make this a fun, interactive dining experience.
  - Where to Try: Kang Ho Dong Baekjeong (Address: 3465 W 6th St, Los Angeles, CA 90020). Known for its high-quality meats and great vibe.

In-N-Out Burger: While not unique in terms of a gourmet experience, In-N-Out is an LA institution. You can't visit without grabbing a Double-Double or animal-style fries.

Where to Try: In-N-Out (Address: 7009 Sunset Blvd, Los Angeles, CA 90028).

Hidden Gems for Great Food Experiences:

- Grand Central Market: Located in Downtown LA, this bustling food hall offers a variety of international and local eats. You can try everything from ramen to Mexican street food.
  - Where to Try: Grand Central Market (Address: 317 S Broadway, Los Angeles, CA 90013). Don't miss Eggslut for amazing egg sandwiches.

- Smorgasburg LA: Every Sunday, this open-air food market hosts a wide range of vendors selling everything from fried chicken sandwiches to gourmet donuts.
    - Where to Try: Smorgasburg LA (Address: 777 S Alameda St, Los Angeles, CA 90021).

Little Ethiopia: If you're in the mood for something unique, Little Ethiopia offers delicious Ethiopian cuisine with communal eating using injera (a spongy flatbread).

Where to Try: Dahlak (Address: 4708 W. Washington Blvd., Los Angeles, CA 90016).

Dining Tips

Whether you're in San Francisco or Los Angeles, there are some essential dining tips to make your food experiences more enjoyable:

Food Festivals and Events:

- San Francisco:

San Francisco Street Food Festival: A great event to experience the city's best food trucks and street vendors. It usually happens in August.

Eat Drink SF: A must for food lovers, this festival brings together top chefs from the Bay Area, offering tastings and culinary events. Typically held in late summer.

- Los Angeles:
    - LA Food and Wine Festival: One of the best food events in LA, featuring local and international chefs, wine tastings, and unique dining experiences. Held every summer.

Taco Festival: If you're a taco lover, don't miss LA's Taco Festival—a celebration of all things tacos, from street vendors to high-end chefs. Usually takes place in June.

Practical Tips for Dining:

- Reservations: Many of LA's and San Francisco's popular restaurants require reservations, especially on weekends. Use apps like OpenTable or check the restaurant's website to secure your spot in advance.

Best Time for Budget-Friendly Dining: Dining out during off-peak hours (early dinner or late lunch) can help you avoid long waits and sometimes get better deals. Lunch menus tend to be more affordable, especially in restaurants offering prix-fixe options.

Tipping: Tipping is customary in both cities. 15-20% of your total bill is standard in both cities. For food trucks or casual dining, tipping is also appreciated but not mandatory.

- Street Food: In both cities, food trucks offer an affordable and authentic way to enjoy local food. Always bring cash, though most trucks also accept credit cards via apps like Square.

Budgeting Food Costs:

San Francisco: Dining can be expensive, especially in touristy areas like Fisherman's Wharf or Union Square. To save money, try visiting neighborhoods like The Mission District or Chinatown, where you can find affordable and authentic food.

Los Angeles: While LA has its upscale restaurants, you can also find plenty of affordable food in markets or food trucks. Downtown LA and Echo Park offer many budget-friendly options.

Part V: Itineraries

Itineraries

Whether you have a few days or an entire week, these itineraries will help you make the most of your time in San Francisco and Los Angeles. From iconic sights to hidden gems, these plans strike a balance between sightseeing, relaxation, and exploring each city's unique character.

3-Day Itinerary for San Francisco

Day 1: Classic San Francisco

- Morning: Start your day with breakfast at Boudin Bakery at Fisherman's Wharf (Address: 160 Jefferson St, San Francisco, CA 94133). Enjoy their famous sourdough bread with a bowl of clam chowder.

- Mid-Morning: Visit the Golden Gate Bridge. Walk or bike across it for stunning views of the city and the bay. Crissy Field offers an excellent vantage point if you prefer to stay on the shore.

- Afternoon: Explore Alcatraz Island. Take the ferry from Pier 33 and enjoy the tour of the infamous prison. It's a fascinating look into the history of this notorious facility.

- Evening: Head to North Beach for dinner at a local Italian restaurant, such as The Stinking

Rose (Address: 325 Columbus Ave, San Francisco, CA 94133), and enjoy the nightlife.

Day 2: Culture and Local Favorites

- Morning: Have breakfast in the Mission District. Visit Tartine Bakery (Address: 600 Guerrero St, San Francisco, CA 94110) for fresh pastries.

- Mid-Morning: Spend time at the SFMOMA (San Francisco Museum of Modern Art) (Address: 151 3rd St, San Francisco, CA 94103) and explore their collection of contemporary works.

- Afternoon: Take a stroll through Golden Gate Park and visit the California Academy of Sciences (Address: 55 Music Concourse Dr, San Francisco, CA 94118) for an interactive experience with the natural world.

- Evening: Explore Chinatown (Address: Chinatown, San Francisco, CA 94108) for authentic Chinese cuisine. R&G Lounge (Address: 631 Kearny St, San Francisco, CA 94108) is a popular choice for classic dishes like salt and pepper crab.

Day 3: Off-the-Beaten-Path & Relaxation

- Morning: Start your day at Dolores Park (Address: 19th St & Dolores St, San

Francisco, CA 94114), where you can relax and people-watch.

- Mid-Morning: Visit the Mission District's street art scene, particularly the colorful murals on Balmy Alley (Address: Balmy Alley, San Francisco, CA 94110).

- Afternoon: For a quieter and less touristy experience, head to Lands End (Address: Point Lobos Ave & El Camino del Mar, San Francisco, CA 94121) for an afternoon hike with beautiful ocean views and historical sites.

- Evening: Wind down at The Ferry Building Marketplace (Address: 1 Ferry Building, San Francisco, CA 94111), where you can sample local goods and enjoy dinner from farm-to-table restaurants.

3-Day Itinerary for Los Angeles

Day 1: Iconic LA

- Morning: Start your day with breakfast at The Griddle Café (Address: 7916 Sunset Blvd, Los Angeles, CA 90046), known for its decadent pancakes.

- Mid-Morning: Head to Hollywood Walk of Fame (Address: Hollywood Blvd, Los Angeles, CA 90028) to see the stars. Take a tour of the TCL Chinese Theatre (Address: 6925 Hollywood Blvd, Los Angeles, CA 90028) for an inside look at this historic landmark.

- Afternoon: Visit Griffith Observatory (Address: 2800 E Observatory Rd, Los Angeles, CA 90027) for panoramic views of the city and the Hollywood Sign.

- Evening: Have dinner in West Hollywood at The Bazaar by José Andrés (Address: 465 La Cienega Blvd, Los Angeles, CA 90048) for an upscale dining experience.

Day 2: Art, Culture & Nature

- Morning: Enjoy breakfast at Grand Central Market (Address: 317 S Broadway, Los Angeles, CA 90013), where you can sample a variety of breakfast foods.

- Mid-Morning: Spend the morning exploring The Getty Center (Address: 1200 Getty Center Dr, Los Angeles, CA 90049). The museum offers incredible art collections, beautiful gardens, and stunning architecture.

- Afternoon: Head to Santa Monica Pier (Address: 200 Santa Monica Pier, Santa Monica, CA 90401) for a fun afternoon of beach activities, shopping, and dining.

- Evening: Dine at The Lobster (Address: 1602 Ocean Ave, Santa Monica, CA 90401) for fresh seafood with views of the ocean.

Day 3: Hidden Gems & Local Flavor

- Morning: Visit The Last Bookstore (Address: 453 S Spring St, Los Angeles, CA 90013), a quirky and unique bookstore perfect for book lovers.

- Mid-Morning: Explore the murals and street art in Downtown LA's Arts District (Address: Los Angeles, CA 90013).

- Afternoon: Take a stroll through the Los Angeles County Museum of Art (LACMA) (Address: 5905 Wilshire Blvd, Los Angeles, CA 90036) and check out the Urban Light installation.

- Evening: For a laid-back dinner, head to Little Ethiopia (Address: 4708 W Washington Blvd, Los Angeles, CA 90016) for delicious Ethiopian cuisine and traditional injera.

1-Week Itinerary for Both Cities

Day 1-3: San Francisco

- Day 1: Arrive in San Francisco. Start with Fisherman's Wharf and visit Pier 39 and

Alcatraz Island. In the evening, dine in North Beach.

- Day 2: Explore Golden Gate Park, the California Academy of Sciences, and SFMOMA. End the day with dinner in Chinatown.

- Day 3: Take a relaxing morning at Dolores Park and explore Mission District murals. Spend the afternoon hiking Lands End and enjoy dinner at The Ferry Building Marketplace.

Day 4-7: Los Angeles

- Day 4: Travel to Los Angeles. Visit Hollywood Walk of Fame, Griffith Observatory, and TCL Chinese Theatre. Enjoy dinner in West Hollywood.

- Day 5: Explore The Getty Center, then head to Santa Monica for beach time and shopping.

- Day 6: Discover LACMA, enjoy street art in the Arts District, and take a trip to Grand Central Market for lunch.

- Day 7: Spend the day in Venice Beach exploring the boardwalk and local art. End your trip with a visit to The Last Bookstore and dinner in Downtown LA.

Travel Planners & Maps.

LA Travel Planner Planner

Month of:

Sun	Mon	Tues	Wed	Thurs	Fri	Sat

You can scan QR code view
San Francisco Maps

Printed in Great Britain
by Amazon